IN HIS OWN WORDS: CHARLES ORR RYAN

THE STORY OF A WW I AMERICAN SOLDIER

As Expressed Through His Letters and Told to His Daughter, Patricia Jane Ryan

BY PATRICIA JANE RYAN AND MARY CATHERINE DAVIS

This publication contains the opinions and ideas of its author. It is intended to provide helpful and informative material on the subjects addressed in the publication. The author and publisher specifically disclaim all responsibility for any liability, loss or risk, personal or otherwise, which is incurred as a consequence, directly or indirectly, of the use and application of any of the contents of this book.

WORKBOOK PRESS LLC
187 E Warm Springs Rd,
Suite B285, Las Vegas, NV 89119, USA

Website: https://workbookpress.com/
Hotline: 1-888-818-4856
Email: admin@workbookpress.com

Ordering Information:
Quantity sales. Special discounts are available on quantity purchases by corporations, associations, and others.
For details, contact the publisher at the address above.

Library of Congress Control Number:
ISBN-13:   978-1-961845-72-5 (Paperback Version)
                978-1-961845-72-5 (Digital Version)

REV. DATE: 08/30/2022

In His Own Words:
Charles Orr Ryan

The Story of a WWI American Soldier

Charles Ryan 1918

CONTENTS

Charles and Bertha, with Jane and Jim 1938

To Jane's parents, Charles and Bertha

and to her siblings

Donald, Marian, Robert, and James

To Cathy's sister, Jo Ann,

for giving Cathy a love of history,

and for teaching her how to write.

Jane and Cathy especially want to thank God

for the opportunity to work together

to share the story of Jane's father,

Charles Ryan

A special mention

To Jane's nephew, Michael Ryan

for realizing that he shared a connection

with his grandfather by both being skillful builders.

WWI uniforms given to soldiers piece by piece

FACTS ABOUT WORLD WAR ONE

- WWI was fought in Europe from 1914-1918

- ONE OF THE MAIN CAUSES: European countries wanted to regain territories lost in previous conflicts, and to build empires.

- The start of WWI began with the assassination of Archduke Ferdinand of Austria-Hungary by a Serbian on June 28, 1914.

- The countries that fought on the side of the Allied Forces included; Britain, France, Russia, Italy, and the United States.

- The countries that fought against the Allies were the Central Powers that included; Germany, Austria-Hungary, Ottoman Empire, and Bulgaria.

- On May 7, 1915, the British passenger ship, Lusitania, was sunk by a torpedo from a German submarine. 1,195 civilian passengers were killed. There were 128 Americans included among the dead.

- Germany later threatened to sink any ship headed for British ports.

- The United States entered WWI on April 6, 1917, when President Woodrow Wilson declared war on the Central Powers as a result of the outrage over the Lusitania incident.

- WWI is one of the deadliest wars ever fought. Civilian and military deaths totaled approximately 18 million people, including 11 million military personnel. It is estimated that there were 23 million wounded.

- There was a devastating loss of land. Buildings, farms, homes, shrines, and natural resources were destroyed on both sides of the conflict.

- WWI was the first time that aircrafts became a significant factor in war.

- Aerial photography was used for reconnaissance and was instrumental in the outcome of the war.

- Fighting ended on November 11, 1918, referred to as Armistice Day.

- The war officially ended with the signing of The Treaty of Versailles in June of 1919 between Germany and the Allied Powers.

- The treaty required Germany to take responsibility for the war and pay reparations. Germany was also required to give up territory. The German people were demoralized.

- WWI was often referred to as "The Great War," or "The War to End All Wars."

*The sources are cited in the bibliography.

Jane's Uncle Nelse , 1918

INTRODUCTION

This book is not about a war. It is about a warrior, Charles Orr Ryan, a soldier in WWI. *In His Own Words* is based on his letters and stories about being sent to the European War Front as a U.S. soldier in the early years of the 20th century. He was an eyewitness during a significant period of American and world history. Through his writing, he created a verbal picture of what he saw, experienced, and thought.

Jane Ryan, a retired teacher, and Charles' youngest daughter, recently came into possession of the letters. She read the letters to another retired teacher, Cathy Davis. Sharing the letters of Charles was a very moving experience for Jane and Cathy. Charles wrote with such clear, descriptive language that his experiences and feelings could be seen and felt through his words. For Jane, reading the letters brought back memories of the discussions she had with her father about the war, before he passed away. The stories her father told her could now be put in context with the letters to create an image of a young man bravely facing the challenges of being sent off to war. Jane became acutely aware that the qualities of the young man from a hundred years ago were reflected in the man she knew as her father. As a labor of love for her parents and family, Jane wanted to share her father's story with the current generation of the Ryan family and their descendants.

Taking into consideration the delicacy of Charles' letters, it became necessary to determine the best method of sharing them. Jane and Cathy decided that it was most important to preserve the essence of Charles' words by quoting him extensively while providing a narrative, forming his words into his story. The book emerged from the realization that Charles' words deserved to be treasured and maintained with honor. Jane and Cathy hope that the purpose of this endeavor has been accomplished.

PART ONE

United States Military Drafts Charles Orr Ryan into World War One

Margie Ryan Boatz sent Jane the letters found in the attic of the family farm house.

"Guess the boys are getting drafted pretty fast up there. Surely will make it pretty hard for the farmers."

(Letter to his mother, May 12, 1918)

Charles Orr Ryan was born on May 7, 1895, on the family farm in St. Vincent, Minnesota. He passed away on August 23, 1983, in Redondo Beach, California. His wife was Bertha (Erickson) Ryan. Charles and Bertha were the parents of eight children. Of the eight children, Donald, Marian, Bob, Jim, and Jane survived to adulthood. Charles was drafted into the United States Army in April 1918 to fight in World War I.

A few months before Charles passed away, he began to tell his daughters, Jane and Marian, some stories about his World War I experience. The following stories are a combination of Jane's reminiscences of her father's recollections, and direct quotations from her father's letters to his family. The letters were recently found by Charles' niece, Margie (Ryan) Boltz, in the attic of the family farmhouse.

Unfortunately, the letters Charles wrote Bertha, his future wife, no longer exist.

When he received his draft notice, Charles was living and working on the farm in St. Vincent, Minnesota. Charles began his Basic Training in Pennsylvania and was then sent to Long Island, New York to complete his training before being shipped out to England. Charles, like so many of the other young men drafted into service during World War I, found himself in environments very different from the farm and small town from which he came.

Longing to remain close to his family, Charles began writing letters.

His letters indicated how much he missed his loved ones. He wanted to know how each member of his family and Bertha was doing. He felt sorry that he wasn't able to help with the crops. "Guess the boys are getting drafted pretty fast up there. Sure will make it pretty hard for the farmers." (May 12, 1918) He kept trying to make connections with his cousin, Cliff, and any of the men he knew from back home. He wrote of his disappointment in not finding anyone from his area.

In a letter to his sister, Ethel, Charles wrote about the stress and tedium of life in the camp. "I haven't had much time to myself these last weeks. They have something for fingerprints, another to sign the payroll, and so on. It's not hard work but it's tiresome cause they line us up and we have to stand and stand until our turn comes up. Sometimes a couple of hours and you know how tiresome that can be until your turn comes." (May 18, 1918)

In Pittsburg, Pennsylvania, Charles was able to get passes allowing him to walk to baseball games and church socials. He even attended some New York Giant games. He always made sure that he would return to camp before his curfew so that he would never get kitchen duty.

During the daytime at camp, Charles and his fellow soldiers trained for war. Most of the farm boys knew how to shoot rifles, but knew nothing of war. One day a unit came to camp and demonstrated marching drills, which amazed them, as they had never seen marching in step like that. Before long, he was learning to march in unison with his group. The soldiers were told always to look straight ahead, not to the left or right. When two soldiers forgot and looked to the right, the whole unit went off the road. The two soldiers disappeared and were never seen by the unit again. (May 18, 1918)

As time passed at training camp, the men had to wait a long

time to get their complete uniforms. The uniforms came to them piece by piece. The last piece of the uniform the men received was the leggings. Charles described in his letters how he did not feel like a real soldier until his uniform was complete. "Just got our uniforms and the leggings haven't arrived yet, so not a real soldier today." (May 26, 1918)

Before he was sent overseas, Charles was transferred to Long Island, New York. Charles wrote that his new address would be:

Replacement Detachment at Garden City

Long Island, New York

Charles wrote how he and the other men were aware that they could be pulled out, placed in squadrons, and sent overseas at any time. "50,000 men left New York Harbor, last Saturday." He described how training continued in the New York camp with more intensity. "We spent a lot of time marching. Some officers came and observed 10,000 men marching to a band. As a result, the officers said that we were the best-skilled men that ever came into camp." (June 23, 1918)

Charles wrote many of his letters to his parents, Myra and Frank Ryan

*Review of the troops, 86 Division, Rockford, Illinois,
April 12, 1918*

When Charles received his leggings,
his uniform was complete.

Uncle Nelse in full uniform.

The men were given projects that identified strengths to determine placement in squadrons. Charles' assignments dealt with patterns. "I am still making patterns. I had to make a pattern by Monday morning. It took me all day." (May 18, 1918). Probably due to his performance on the assigned tasks, Charles was later placed in the Air Squadron and sent to aircraft school overseas. He was trained to build airplanes out of wood. He was classified as a carpenter.

While he was in the New York camp, the flu epidemic of 1918 took the lives of many of the recruits. The recruits were living together in large tents. Charles was assigned the job of carrying the dead bodies out of the tent. He was afraid to catch the disease and he dreaded each day of the assignment. However, he did as he was told. Throughout his basic training, Charles never got to visit New York City. (Related to Jane, 1982)

In basic training, Charles wrote about his concerns for the future.

There were three hundred thirty draftees in his unit from Minnesota. Every day men would be shipped out. None of the men, including Charles, knew when they would be sent overseas. "I am still waiting to be called up."

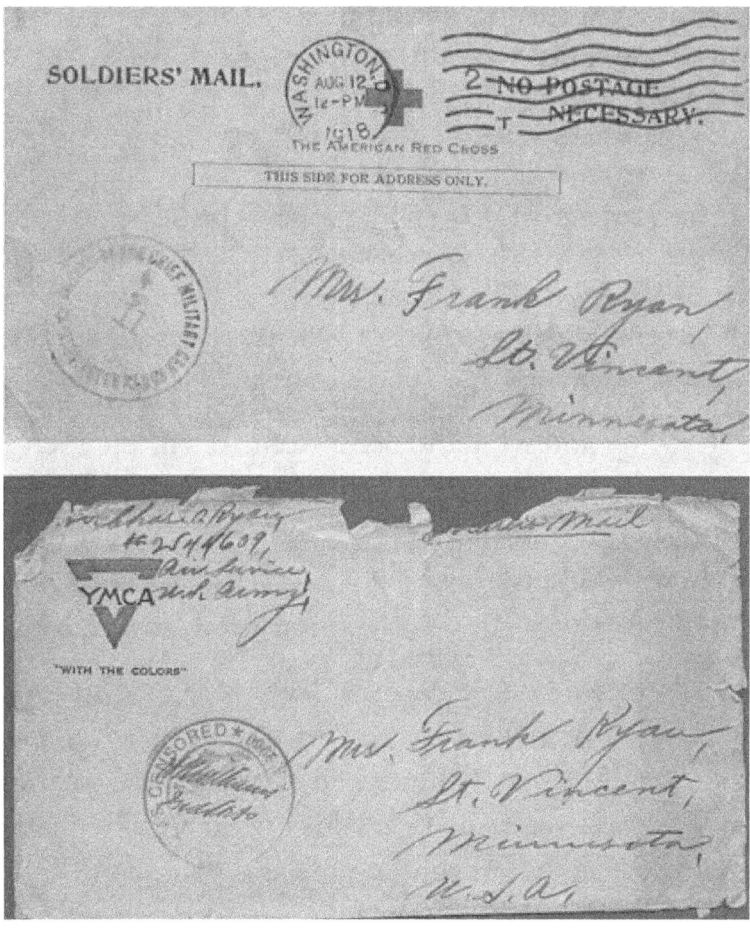

*The YMCA provided personal comforts,
including stationarey.*

"I can't figure out why some are going and some aren't. How are they selecting them? Seems to be based on the squadron they are being put in." (July 7, 1918)

Soon he wrote home that he was being shipped out to London England with 50 other men from his unit. He was given a postcard to address and sign informing his family about his safe arrival when he landed in England. He was told that he could not have any other communication with his family until after he was in England. He was ordered not to ever give any other information about his trip across the ocean. He followed orders until a few months before he passed away, when he told his daughters, Jane and Marian, about some of his experiences.

Charles described how he left on a small cattle ship. He could not believe how big and wide the ocean seemed. All the men became very seasick. A few days before the ship arrived in England, the ship was going to be attacked. The men believed that they would not be alive in the morning.

Fortunately, huge wind and storm came along at night. Charles was amazed to see huge waves that were at least thirty feet high. The men were tossed all over the ship. By daybreak, the ship had lost the subs. The ship was unharmed. The next day, Charles found out that the two other American ships were sunk by the German subs during the night (As told to Jane and Marian, 1983).

"I arrived August 4th/. I sent a postcard from the ship. See my new address on the post, (211th Aero Squadron, American Expeditionary Forces). As long as you don't hear anything of me, you will know I'm alright because if anything should happen, they'll let you know right away." (August 4, 1918)

Many types of ships were used to transport soldiers.
Jane's Uncle Nelse returned from France on this ship.

Assembly of soldiers being sent to war,
Bristol, Belguim.
(August 8, 1918)

In his letters, Charles did not give specific information about his location or his trip across the ocean. "We arrived somewhere in England." In his description of his trip, he never mentioned the story or how seasick the men were, or the near-tragic encounter with the German subs. What he did write was that he never thought that the ocean was so wide "…water, water, everywhere" (August 4, 1918). All his letters were read and signed by official censors. Any potentially strategic information was blackened out or cut out of the letters.

Charles' feelings of loneliness and his desire to know about his home are expressed even more seriously in his letters from England. He wrote on August 8, 1918, that he kept "looking for mail". However, his mail did not arrive for several weeks. In the remainder of his August 8th letter, he wrote about his thoughts of home and his impressions of England.

"Suppose everybody is busy harvesting these days. Wouldn't mind taking a look at good old Minnesota crops. It (England) is a nice country. Swell looking places. Quite Hilly. A lot of cattle because the pastures are on the hillsides. Lots of nice trees. Cool and raining an awful lot." (August 8, 1918)

At the end of his August 8th letter, Charles said that he was going to school to learn to be a carpenter. He would be building airplane wings made out of wood. He was assigned to a location next to an airfield. He would often go out to watch the airplanes taking off. The letter also described how the American and the English camps were side-by-side.

Each country had its airfield. Each camp was connected to a YMCA in which the men could go for bathing and relaxation activities. (August 8, 1918)

In a conversation Charles had with Jane many years later, Charles told her that there was an empty seat beside the pilot. Many of the non-pilots would go out to observe the take-off and help push the airplanes off the cliffs. Charles said that at the time the men did not realize that in the process of pushing the airplanes off the cliffs, the stirring up of the rocks and dust could result in eye injuries and loss of vision. The pilots often invited the spectators to join the flight in the empty seat. Charles said that no one accepted the offer because some of the airplanes never came back.

Charles was trained to build wooden wings on WWI Airplanes.

Soldiers marching into Belgium, 1917

Charles wrote in his August 8, 1918 letter that he kept up with the war news by reading the British newspapers every morning. "…the papers are full of war news. The Germans are getting hit hard. Hope they keep it up." (August 8, 1918)

On August 17th, Charles wrote "I think that the war will soon be over if we keep driving the Germans the way they have been the last few days." (August 17, 1918)

In Charles' letter of August 25th, he gave a brief description of a soldier's day off from camp. "Went into one of the towns nearby last Thursday, as that was my holiday. Walked for about 5 minutes and then rode on a train a few miles. Got a ride on one of the trucks coming back, so that made it pretty nice. Had a pretty good time but then everything was pretty. Also got weighed, 161 lbs. That's the most I ever weighed.

Gained 20 lbs. since I left there [home]."

Charles Ryan with friend (England)

War slogan on a musical score cover

men we raised, trained, and sent to France; notwithstanding our great efforts in the manufacture of munitions, airplanes, and the other active engines of destruction which, out of our abundant resources, we fashioned for the overthrow of the Hun, food was, after all, our greatest weapon.

"There were some sneers and there was not a little jesting when Herbert Hoover made 'Food Will Win the War' the slogan of the Food Administration, yet food did what Mr. Hoover prophesied it would do. Mr. Hoover himself has several times given testimony to the part played by the hotels of the country in making our great food savings possible. It was the hotels that demonstrated how food could be saved by setting the example, and it was the example of the hotels of the country that led or shamed housewives into doing their own patriotic duty in the homes.

"What the great hotels of the country—the hotels of the better class—did to help win the war has not brought them the credit that is due. In carrying out their pledges to the Food Administration, they suffered actual loss. Charges of profiteering were hurled at them, and when they gave up the use of wheat, the

"Food will win the war."
(Herbert Hoover -
Chairman of the U.S. Food Administration)

PART TWO

AMERICAN EXPEDITIONARY FORCE:

CHARLES ORR RYAN STATIONED IN

ENGLAND

1918

"The Germans are getting hit hard. Guess the papers are full of war news. Hope they keep it up!"

(August 17, 1918)

In his letters home, Charles expressed his frustration with not being home to help on the farm. "Wish I could be home-help with crops. Guess you'll get along somehow." He goes on to describe his daily life at the camp. "I work from 8am to 5pm. Worked one night after supper. Been busy." (August 17, 1918)

The fledging American Air Force was still closely tied to the British Royal Air Squadron. "Got paid in English money. Have to be careful counting the change." (August 17, 1918)

Charles' letters continue to depict his experience and how he coped with his ever-present loneliness. "Be sure to write to me in Garden City. There are two YMCAs here. An American one and a British one. They hold services every Sunday evening. I have been over nearly every Sunday. Makes it pretty nice when you can go over there. They also have books that you can read there." (August 25, 1918)

"I subscribed for the Stars and Strips newspaper. A newspaper published in France. It's only weekly. Have been thinking of sending it to you but will decide later cause it will be pretty old by the time it gets to you." He goes on to write, "London, 60 miles away I'm going next time to London. No mail yet. 10 miles from Oxford. Stopped 3 hours when we arrived. Can get books at the YMCA. Can't send the paper. Can't send anything like that." (September 8, 1918)

Charles, on September 12, 1918, wrote from Weston on the Green, England, "Mail is slow. Got a letter on September 13. It was sent two months ago on July 13th. It is better to get a late letter than none at all. I will be able to build an airplane when I get back. The weather is cold and it has rained for 10 days."

In the September 1918 letters, Charles shares more of his daily routine. "Put a whole month in England. Send me Cliff's address. Don't worry about me. Everything is all right. I am in the best of health at present. 211th Aero Squadron UEF England." (September 1, 1918) "No mail yet. I hope you are well. I work on an airplane every day and on Saturday and Sunday 8am to 5pm. We have an hour for dinner. It has rained every day since September 1st." (September 12, 1918)

On September 18th, Charles refers to the change in the status of the American military air division classification. Charles' mailing address was ordered to reflect the beginning identification of the American Air Force. It is historically significant that Charles was one of the 57, 508 men serving in the American Expeditionary Force (AEF) when the AEF became one of the early incarnations of the American Air Force. (WIKIPEDIA citing GORRELL'S HISTORY OF THE AEF AIR SERVICE 1917 t1919, Vol. 227th Aero Squadrons).

"Address below, AEF doesn't go any longer. Write American out in full."

211th Air Squadron

American Air Force

England

Charles began his September 23rd letter by asking about home. "How is little Margaret? Tell her I expect to be back home before such an awful, awful long time. I went to Oxford Saturday pm and stayed until Sunday afternoon. Oxford is a big university. There are many cottages in town. I got a ride both ways on a truck. Otherwise, I must walk 4 miles to a train at Bissterl. It is just a station and a few little buildings around it." (September 13, 1918)

"Oxford is a pretty fair-sized place. I spent my time nicely. I looked around the University buildings. I got a letter from mother dated September 15th. I'm not getting any mail. I am still building airplane wings. I don't like the climate here. It is damp all the time. It has rained every day since I came. Only 4 or 5 days without rain. Don't write WESTON ON THE GREEN in my address. I'm just here today. Can't tell where I'll be in a few days."

Throughout his time of deployment, Charles incorporates news of the progress of the war in his letters. In his September 25th letter, Charles writes "We are taking lots of prisoners. We are driving them back. We are moving out of our tents into our barracks." (September 25, 1918) The contents of the remainder of his October letters weave descriptions of his daily activities with news of the war. "On K.P. (Kitchen Police) I am cooking and washing pans." "Germans, Huns, President Wilson—it didn't take President Wilson long to answer Germany's note." (October 9, 1918)

On October 20th, Charles was selected to go by himself to a

new school for additional training at a different camp. Charles was finally getting lots of mail and newspapers. Charles found out that his cousin Cliff was in London. Charles was hoping that he could use his 7-day leave to find Cliff in London. "I get 7 days for every 4 months overseas. War news is good. Austria is talking about peace. You can't believe them. My friend from Winnipeg was just killed in the war." (October 31, 1918)

Charles toured Oxford on his day off. September 1918

Charles toured Oxford on his day off. September 1918

PART THREE

WORLD WAR ONE
COMES TO AN END

"One big day in England, and the same all over the world."

(Armistice Day letter, November 11, 1918)

November 11, 1918, was the date of the last letter from the bundle of Charles' letters found at the family farmhouse.

November 11, 1918, is also acknowledged and celebrated as Armistice Day, the end of World War One. As usual, Charles's letter reflects the historical news of the day.

"Huns (Germans) signed the Armistice this morning. I guess they'll sign peace terms before too long. I got word about 11am this morning at school. Everything stopped for the rest of the day. We aren't allowed to leave camp for several days, so we are all taking it easy. I went to a small town yesterday. It was called AYLASBURY (population 5,000). It was very quiet in the town. All the towns are like that now. Haven't had the flu yet. They have had their share of it. The worst is over." (November 11, 1918).

The written stories of Charles at war ended. However, many years later, after the death of his wife and shortly before his death, Charles began telling his daughters, Marian and Jane, about some of his experiences. One of the vents Charles shared with Jane happened a few days after the Armistice was signed. Jane, in recalling her father's story, said that she asked her father about how he became classified as DAV (Disabled American Veteran). Charles said that a few days after the Armistice, the soldiers were greeted in the morning by a long line of tables with doctors sitting at each table.

The soldiers were ordered to line up for medical examinations. The purpose was to identify war injuries and other health issues before the troops went home.

When Charles was examined, he was informed that he would be permanently blind in his left eye. The doctors explained that the injury was probably caused by the debris flying around when the fighter airplanes were being pushed off the cliffs. The doctor handed Charles a form stating that Charles would be identified as a DAV for the rest of his life. From that day on, Charles received a small government pension every month, and every year on Armistice Day, he received a red paper poppy. The poppy came from the War Department in remembrance of the soldiers left behind, as immortalized in the poem "In Flanders Field" by John McCrae.

Charles received benefits for partial loss of vision

The symbolic meaning of the read poppy came from the poem "In Flanders Fields" by John McCrae. The poem, written in 1915, was about the soldiers who made the ultimate sacrifice in WWI. The poem has come to be representative of the many different kinds of sacrifice made by our military in many wars.

IN FLANDERS FIELDS

In Flanders Fields, the poppies blow

Between the crosses, row on row,

That mark our place: and in the sky

The larks, still bravely singing, fly

Scarce heard amid the guns below.

We are the dead. Short days ago

We lived, felt drawn, saw sunset glow,

Loved and were loved, and now we lie

In Flanders Fields.

Take up our quarrel with the foe;

To you from falling hands we throw

The torch; be yours to hold it high,

If ye break faith, with us who die

We shall not sleep, though poppies grow

In Flanders Fields.

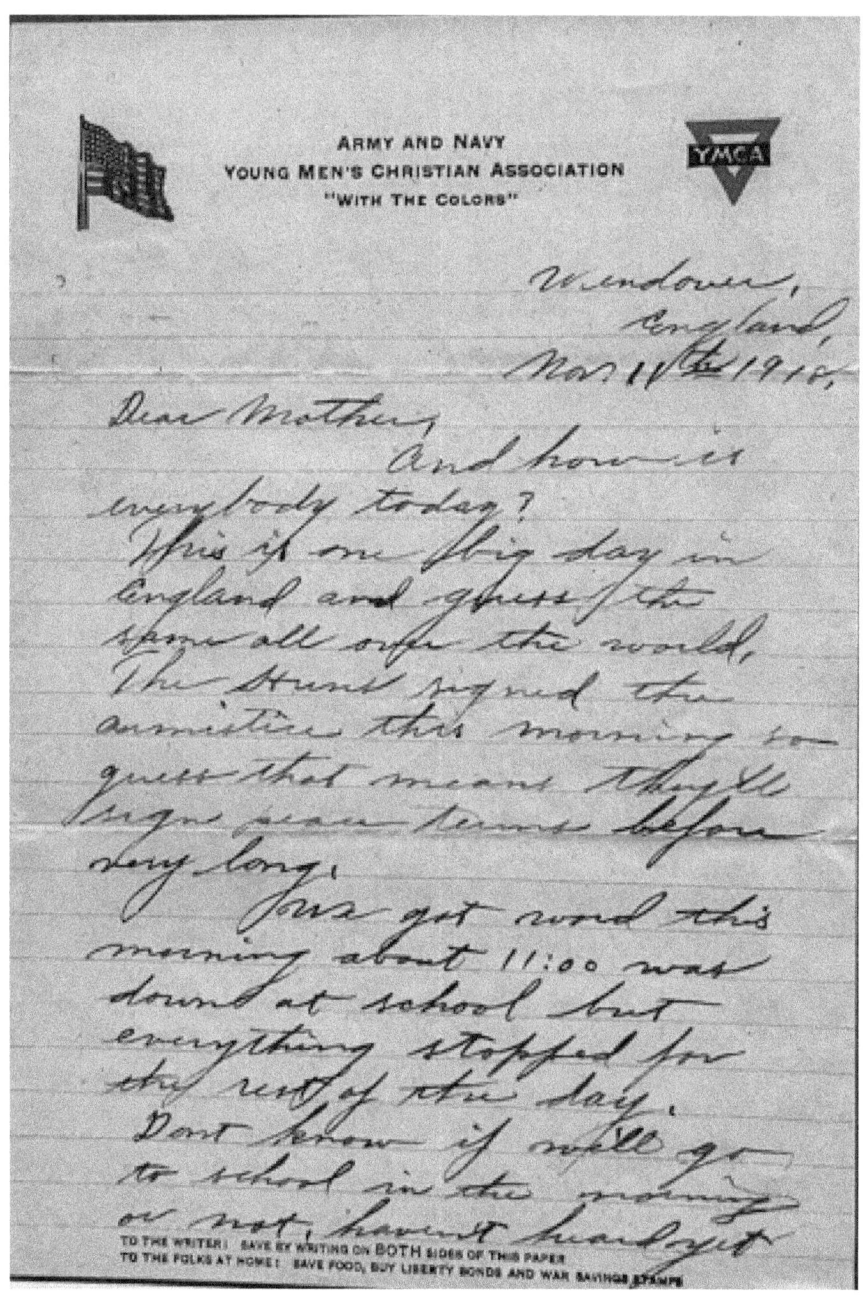

Armistice Letter page 1

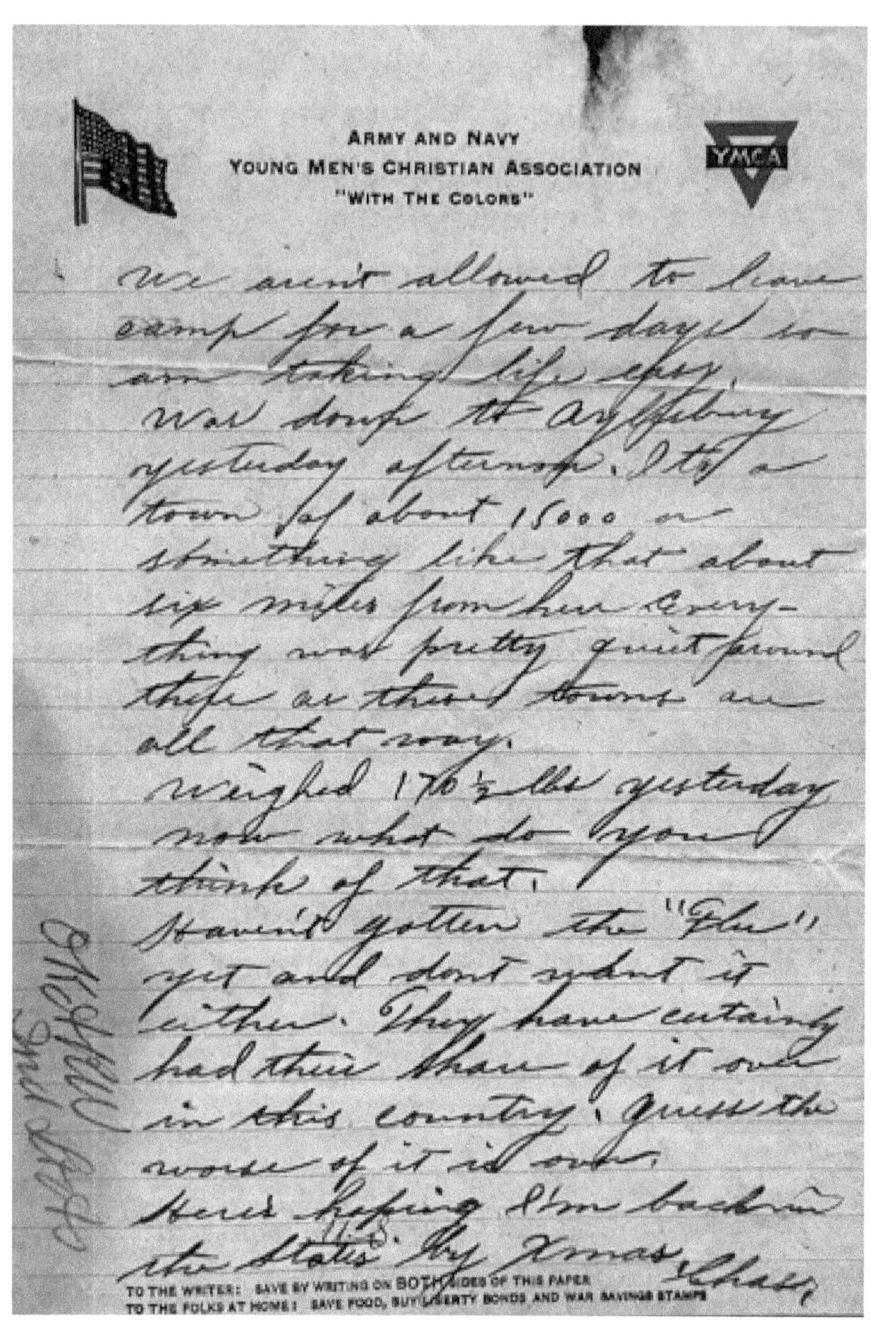

We aren't allowed to leave
camp for a few days so
are taking life easy.
Was down to Aylesbury
yesterday afternoon. It's a
town of about 15000 or
something like that about
six miles from here. Everything was pretty quiet around
there as these towns are
all that way.
Weighed 176½ lbs yesterday
now what do you
think of that.
Haven't gotten the "Flu"
yet and don't want it
either. They have certainly
had their share of it over
in this country. Guess the
worse of it is over.
Here's hoping I'm back in
the states by Xmas.
Chas.

TO THE WRITER: SAVE BY WRITING ON BOTH SIDES OF THIS PAPER.
TO THE FOLKS AT HOME: SAVE FOOD, BUY LIBERTY BONDS AND WAR SAVINGS STAMPS

Armistice Letter page 2

Charles, like many men of his generation, was a very modest man. He never spoke of the "Heroes' Welcome" the soldiers received in their home towns and cities throughout the country. Jane's mother, Bertha, (Charles' wife of 62 years), would sometimes reminisce about a few stories of Charles before they were married. She shared about the excitement in town, all in preparation for the soldier's big parade. Bertha, very proudly, bragged about being the first girl in her town to get a stylish, short haircut. She was getting ready to meet her Charlie.

Bertha was very pleased that Charles was in an early homecoming group. She explained that there was a lottery to determine which soldiers would stay back to bury the dead and to clear up after the war. Bertha's two brothers did not return for a few months.

According to Bertha, the only time that Charles mentioned the war was several years later when he ran into a fellow soldier that was on the same ship going to England. The two men shared memories of their time of service. At one point, Charles asked the man if he remembered how awful the coffee tasted. The man informed Charles that they were given tea, not coffee! After that, there were two things that Charles would refuse to do, drink tea and return to England. (Jane remembers this as her mother's story.)

Charles and Bertha met before Charles was drafted. They were married two years after the war on June 20, 1920. They had eight children. Five of their children grew to adulthood. Jane and Robert are the two remaining survivors. Charles and Bertha were married for many decades. Together they raised their family through the Depression, in wartime, and in peacetime. Charles left the farm and had several jobs in order to support his family. His final position was as a representative of the United States Government working with the Disabled American Veterans.

Jane remembers growing up in a loving, supportive family in Chicago. Charles and Bertha can be thought of as ideal representatives of their time. They raised their children with the traditional American values of faith, family, and duty to the country.

Bertha Erickson (1918)

Ryan family, Thanksgiving (1959)

Conclusion

One hundred years separate the daughter reading the World War One letters from the twenty-two-year-old soldier that would one day become her father. For Jane, this was a transcending experience. Jane remembers her father as a definitive role model of the ideal father. He was honorable, dignified, kind, and hard-working. He was devoted to his family. He was also a reserved and modest man. He rarely spoke about his personal feelings and experiences.

Before Charles and Bertha were married, they made an agreement that Charles would be the provider and Bertha would be in charge of the home. As man and wife, they proudly kept their agreement. They also kept their private life and their personal concerns to themselves. They were parents. They gave support and guidance. They did not share their thoughts and feelings. It is for these reasons that reading the letters of the young man expressing himself so openly gave Jane a more intimate understanding of her father than she ever imagined.

It was the main purpose of Jane and Cathy to tell the story of Charles in World War One. In the process of going through the experience of pursuing this objective, Jane and Cathy realized that Charles, in his letters, brought a voice to many young soldiers who have been sent away from home to a foreign land to risk their lives in service to their country.

In today's society, the soldiers who fought in World War I are seldom acknowledged, and few movies are made about World War I. The men who fought in that war are not considered part of "The Greatest Generation." Yet, these men deserve to be recognized for the sacrifice they made. The story told by the letters Charles wrote brings light to their sacrifice.

As a fitting tribute to the generational difference between Charles serving his country as a soldier at war, and Charles as a father caring for his wife and family, the words of Ecclesiastes 3 seem appropriate.

There is an appointed time for everything,
And a time for every affair under the heavens.

And a time to give birth, and a time to die;
A time to plant, and a time to uproot the plant.

A time to kill, and a time to heal;
A time to tear down, and a time to build.

A time to weep, and a time to laugh;
A time to mourn, and a time to dance.

A time to scatter stones, and a time to gather them;
A time to embrace, and a time to be far from embraces.

A time to seek, and a time to lose;
A time to keep, and a time to cast away.

A time to rend, and a time to sew;
A time to be silent, and a time to speak.

A time to love, and a time to hate;
A time of war, and a time of peace.

(Source: New American Bible)

Acknowledgments

Jane and Cathy would like to express their appreciation to the following individuals for the valuable assistance given to them to complete this work:

To Jane's cousin Margie Ryan-Boltz for her generosity and thoughtfulness in realizing how much these letters would be treasured by Jane.

To Annie Appel, noted artist, author, and photographer, for her willingness to offer her expertise in photography, and her experience in preparing materials for publication. Annie's encouragement, warmth, and valuable advice made it possible for Jane and Cathy to achieve what seemed to be an impossible goal.

To Diane Cooper, a dear friend, who willingly gave her time to help edit several drafts of the text.

To Joey Davis, Cathy's nephew, for organizing our text which was scattered in many parts in two computers in different programs. To Cathy's nephew, Alex Davis, for teaching Cathy how to use the writing program on her new computer. To Kim Nikkoli Gelua, for patiently helping Jane and Cathy deal with modern technology.

To Kayla Ryyth, a talented art student, for her authentic, detailed sketches of a World War One uniform. To Gary Ryyth, Kayla's father for his beautiful drawing of a World War One fighter airplane. Talent obviously runs in the family.

To Sister Mary Catherine McShane, head of the History Department of the University of San Diego College for Women during the late 60's and early 70's, who required Mary Catherine Davis to do many hours of agonizing research on primary sources. She would have loved these letters!

BIBLIOGRAPHY

Flood, Charles Bracelen. First To Fly. New York; Grove Press, 2015.

World War One Facts. www.ifacts.net. "World War One Timeline 1914-1918". Accessed November 26, 2017.

World War One Casualties (Estimated) Nadeoe Mougel@ CVCE-2011.2011 REPERES EUNET.

U.S., World War One Draft Registration Card, 1917-1918 National Archives and Record Administration

Documentary Film: "The First World War From Above" DIRECTOR: Mark Radice. Publishers: BBC, 2010